Greek Mythology:

Ancient Myths and Classic Stories – The Complete Guide

JEREMIAH STEVENS

Copyright © 2016 Jeremiah Stevens

All rights reserved.

© **Copyright 2016 - All rights reserved.**

In no way is it legal to reproduce, duplicate, or transmit any part of this document in either electronic means or in printed format. Recording of this publication is strictly prohibited and any storage of this document is not allowed unless with written permission from the publisher. All rights reserved.

The information provided herein is stated to be truthful and consistent, in that any liability, in terms of inattention or otherwise, by any usage or abuse of any policies, processes, or directions contained within is the solitary and utter responsibility of the recipient reader. Under no circumstances will any legal responsibility or blame be held against the publisher for any reparation, damages, or monetary loss due to the information herein, either directly or indirectly.

Respective authors own all copyrights not held by the publisher.

Legal Notice:

This book is copyright protected. This is only for personal use. You cannot amend, distribute, sell, use, quote or paraphrase any part or the content within this book without the consent of the author or copyright owner. Legal action will be pursued if this is breached.

Disclaimer Notice:

Please note the information contained within this document is for educational and entertainment purposes only. Every attempt has been made to provide accurate, up to date and reliable complete information. No warranties of any kind are expressed or implied. Readers acknowledge that the author is not engaging in the rendering of legal, financial, medical or professional advice.

By reading this document, the reader agrees that under no circumstances are we responsible for any losses, direct or indirect, which are incurred as a result of the use of information contained within this document, including, but not limited to, —errors, omissions, or inaccuracies.

TABLE OF CONTENTS

Introduction

Chapter One - Sources of Greek Mythology

Chapter Two – The Primeval Gods

Chapter Four - Giants and Cyclops

Chapter Five – The Olympian Gods

Chapter Six - Other Important Gods

Chapter Seven - Hercules

Chapter Eight - Jason And The Argonauts

Conclusion

Introduction

Mythology has been a constant source of inspiration for all cultures. Each civilization around the world have developed a collection of myths, legends and folk-stories which explain the world around them, from where the wind comes to how there are certain types of plants and even what happens after death. However, there is no doubt that the myths of ancient Greece are unsurpassed. The myths of the ancient Greeks have fascinated and enthralled millions throughout the centuries, from politicians to philosophers to artists, poets, writers and movie producers. Even today, the myths of ancient Greece continue to importance and relevance in modern society.

There are a number of different types of myths. Religious myths focus on the gods and heroes or are related to specific religious ceremonies and rites. These include the legends concerning how the world was formed out of chaos, the rulers of the cosmos and the various wars between the Titans and the younger Olympian gods, including that of Zeus. In addition to this, the countless love affairs of Zeus, Poseidon, Hermes, Apollo and other gods are included in this category as these love affairs usually resulted in the birth of other gods and heroes. For example, the stories which feature Apollo's victories portray his jealous nature and the danger that comes about when you make deals with the gods. When it comes to Dionysus, however, his myths show the hostility which emerges by a new religion. A number of the myths concerning Greek heroes will have a religious foundation.

Legends are a little different compared to myths. Myths are the stories which embody sacred or religious beliefs, but legends (also known as sagas) are considered to have a historical background, or at least a grain of historical truth to them. For example, the Trojan War and the voyage of Jason and the Argonauts are believed to really have happened and the heroes were actual living beings (however, it should be stressed that the events would be very different compared to the stories told in the legends). The Trojan War was believed to have occurred a few centuries before Homer created his famous poem, *The Iliad*, and archaeological evidence in modern day Turkey supports this theory. Many of the ancient Greek legends are full of rich accounts of divine intervention, but scholars believe there was a true historical basis to them.

Legends were also used to provide a basis for political purposes, social control, a way to explain taking over new territory and science as well as entertainment. For example, raping a goddess or trying to trick the gods meant that after death you would be punished forever in the underworld. This meant that the general public could be controlled in regards to punishment; allowing the legends to mirror Greek society.

A third type of story is referred to as folktales. Folktales usually consist of someone who has lost someone or is lost themselves and then found after a series of adventures. Some of the major characters from these types of stories can include Paris of Troy, Helen, Orpheus, Heracles (also known as Hercules), Odysseus, Theseus etc. These are stories where the main character typically overcomes all obstacles and finally wins the day by using cunning and bravery. These types of stories were incredibly popular with the ancient Greek audience, as well as today's audience.

Many other themes can be found throughout Greek mythology – wicked stepmothers, tyrant fathers, beautiful princesses needing to be rescued by monstrous creatures and memory loss are featured in many stories, with the hero or main character overcoming them all.

Chapter One - Sources of Greek Mythology

The Homeric Poems: *The Iliad* and the *Odyssey*

Two of the most famous poems in the world, known as *the Iliad* and the *Odyssey* are attributed to an 8th or 9th century BCE poet named Homer. Homer is one of two of ancient Greece's earliest writers which tell of the gods. *The Iliad* concerns the story of the Trojan War whereas the *Odyssey* tells of Odysseus' 10 year journey home to Ithaca after the end of the Trojan War. From these poems we know that the audience would know the myths and characters, highlighting the fact that the gods and heroes were well known and already established centuries earlier.

Hesiod: The *Theogony* and *Works and Days*

Hesiod is one of the greatest poets from ancient Greece and from the *Theogony* and *Works and Days* gives us a great deal of information on the gods and how they were perceived by society at the time. Hesiod lived in the 8th century BCE, around the same time as Homer, and gives us many myths and legends. Whilst both works are very different, they are considered at times to be a diptych, depending on each other.

Other literary works

Whilst *The Iliad* gives us our best knowledge on the Trojan War, there are a number of gaps and holes in it and, as such, there are a number of fragments from before Homer that helps us fill in these holes. The Homeric Hymns, which are shorter poems, present numerous religious myths. Then we have several lyric poets including Pindar of Thebes (6th -5th century BCE) as well as Aeschylus, Euripides and Sophocles from later in the 5th century

BCE, all of whom give us a rich source of information concerning the gods and heroes.

During the Hellenistic period (323 – 30 BCE) a number of writers emerged. These include the works of Callimachus from Alexandria who wrote down many of the lesser known stories. At the same time we have Euhemerus who put forth the theory that the gods were once humans – this theory eventually was referred to as Euhemerism. The best version of the legend of Jason and the Argonauts was from Apollonius of Rhodes.

A number of invaluable sources of ancient mythology come from the period of the Roman Empire. These include Geography from Strabo, who dates from the 1st century BCE; Apollodorus' *Library* in the 2nd century CE; the works of Plutarch; the *Latin Genealogies* of Hyginus; and from the 2nd century CE historian, Pausanias.

Chapter Two – The Primeval Gods

The primeval gods were the first gods to emerge out of nothing. Known as the Protogenoi, they were the personifications of the cosmos when the universe was created. The majority of these deities were elemental deities, being the representations of the world instead of a physical being. For example, Gaea was the earth, Uranus the sky and Oceanus the world's water. However, when they were depicted in a more human way, they were seen as half a person rising from their native element (i.e. Gaea from the earth or Thalassa rising from the oceans).

Gaea

Also known as Gaia or Ge, Gaea was the female personification of the earth and the mother and wife of Uranus. She was the mother of many of the Titans, the giants, the Erinyes and the Cyclopes. From archaeology and linguistics, it appears as though Gaea was a mother goddess worshipped in Greece long before the Olympian gods were introduced by the Hellenes. She continued to be the great mother of the ancient Greeks, although her worship wasn't as far spread during the Hellenistic period.

Nyx

Nyx was the female personification of the night who, according to Homer in *the Iliad*, was feared even by Zeus. In Hesiod's *Theogony*, Nyx was the daughter of Chaos and the mother of many of the primeval forces which included Sleep, Death, Nemesis and the Fates. In other sources, she was the daughter of Phanes, whilst others make her the mother of Uranus by Phanes, Cronus by Uranus and Zeus. She had great oracular powers but whilst her character has been the inspiration for many artists, her worship wasn't as far spread as other gods.

Oceanus

According to Greek mythology, Oceanus was one of the primeval gods and the male personification of the river which circled Gaea, the earth. He was said to live in the west near the location of the Cimmerii, the dark land of dreams, and the gateway to the underworld. According to Hesiod, Oceanus was the eldest Titan and the offspring of Gaea and Uranus, the husband of Tethys and the father of the rivers, streams and the Oceanids, the nymphs of the sea. Homer, however, tells that Oceanus was one of the creator gods, that he begot the gods and even as the creator of all things; although this notion was rare, it was one that was visited by later writers. Oceanus was depicted many times in ancient art, typically as a bearded man.

Ananke

Ananke was the female personification of fate and necessity. She emerged at the beginning of creation, self-forming as an incorporeal serpentine being. The Orphic fragments are the first mentioning of her but even after Homer gives us his accounts of the gods, Ananke was a prominent figure in Greek mythology. Legends tell that when she was born, she emerged with her consort, Khronos, the god of time, wrapped in his serpentine coils. They wrapped their coils around the primeval egg and then spilt it into three – the heavens, the earth and the sea, bringing order to chaos. Ananke was worshipped at Corinth, the only place where we know of, along with Bai, the personification of might or force. Due to her nature, she was not offered sacrifices or gifts since it was useless, as nothing was stronger than necessity. One source makes Ananke the daughter of Hydros and Gaea, as the mother of the Moirai, Chaos, Aether, Phanes and Erebos. There is only one surviving representation of Ananke from antiquity, an Athenian red-figure lekythos vase which depicts the goddess as a lovely woman with wings and holding a torch.

Eros

In Greek mythology, Eros was a primeval god, the offspring of Chaos according to Hesiod, but later writers make him the son of Aphrodite by Zeus, Ares or Hermes. Eros was not simply a god of love, but fertility and the force of such passions. He was the brother of Anteros, the god of reciprocated love, and was sometimes depicted as his adversary. His main attendants were Pothos (Longing) and Himeros (Desire); in Alexandrian poems he was depicted as cute little child with a naughty character; in Archaic art he was portrayed as a handsome young man with wings but by the Hellenistic period, he had changed into a winged baby. Eros was worshipped throughout Greece and the rest of the classical world but his main cult centre was located at Thespiae in Boetia and shared a wall with Aphrodite at the Acropolis in Athens.

Uranus

Uranus was the male personification of the heavens and according to Hesiod, the son of Gaea and her husband. From their union, they created the Titans, the Hecatoncheires and the Cyclops. Uranus was disgusted at the way his sons looked and so locked the Hecatoncheires and the Cyclops deep within the earth. Gaea was angry at the way her children were being treated and so asked her other sons to help. Cronus, along with four of his brothers, devised a plan to overthrow their father. They hid one day and when Uranus descended from the skies to lay with Gaea, they pinned him down, one Titan brother holding an arm or leg, with Cronus in the middle who then castrated Uranus with a scimitar or sickle. The blood from his castrated genitalia fell onto Gaea and formed the Furies, the Giants and the ash tree nymphs called the Meliai. The genitals fell into the ocean and from the sea foam that sprang up from it created Aphrodite, the goddess of love (although other sources say she was the daughter of Zeus).

Uranus prophesized that the Titans would fall just as he did, a prophecy that came about with the birth of Cronus' youngest son, Zeus.

Uranus had no cult centre in Greece and certain features in his myths, such as the sickle or scimitar, suggest that his roots lay in Asia Minor in addition to having a similarity to the Hittite myth of Kumbari.

Chapter Three – The Titans

The Titans were the second generation of Greek gods, the offspring of the primeval gods. They ruled the universe before the Olympian gods gained supremacy. The Titans were the race of gods which organized the universe, establishing a fixed divine cycle in the cosmos and ordering time and the seasons.

After castrating his father, Cronos took charge of the heavens with his sister-wife Rhea but was eventually overthrown and castrated by his own son, Zeus. When the younger Olympian gods finally defeated them, many of the Titans were imprisoned in Tartarus by Zeus, but those who had allied themselves with the Olympians were free. Other Titans, such as Prometheus and Atlas, were given cruel and never-ending punishments when they rebelled against his rule. The female Titans had stayed neutral during the Titan Way and were able to retain their oracular powers. Some of these Titanides (female Titans) engaged in love affairs with Zeus and stayed on Mount Olympus to raise their children.

Atlas

Atlas was the son of Iapetus and the Oceanid goddess Clymene (or Asia by other sources) and was the brother of Prometheus. In Book One of the *Odyssey*, Homer tells that Prometheus was a sea deity who supported the pillars which separated heaven and earth. The location for these were believed to have been placed in the sea just past the horizon in the west, but in later times Atlas was changed to a group of mountains in northwest Africa. One myth tells that Atlas was a king of this region but was transformed into stone by Perseus using the severed head of the Gorgon Medusa. In the *Theogony*, however, Hesiod tells that Atlas was a Titan who fought against Zeus in the Titan War and was punished by bearing the weight of the heavens on his shoulders for all eternity.

In many artworks, Atlas would be depicted as a massive man holding the heavens or holding a globe.

Mnemosyne

Mnemosyne was the Titan goddess of memory. She was the daughter of Uranus and Gaea, and Hesiod tells us she was the mother of the nine Muses (or Younger Muses) by Zeus. According to the myth, Zeus journeyed to Pieria and stayed with Mnemosyne for nine nights and together conceived the beautiful Muses. Mnemosyne was additionally a goddess of time; the female personification of the memorisation required so that stories could be preserved for all eternity before writing was introduced. As such, Mnemosyne became the mother of the Muses, who were patron goddesses of poetry, drama, song etc. As a Titan, Mnemosyne also possessed oracular powers just like her sister Titanides; she was the overseer of the subterranean oracle of Trophonios in Boeotia. Mnemosyne was also regarded as one of the three Elder Muses, the goddesses of music.

Prometheus

Prometheus is one of the most recognizable figures from Greek mythology. He was the Titan god of fire and is famous for tricking or cheating the gods. His name translates as "Forethought" or "Forethinker", stressing his intellect and cunning. Hesiod tells of two legends concerning Prometheus; in one, Prometheus cheats Zeus out of the meat from sacrifices, instead Zeus accepts the bones and fatty parts of the sacrifice. In revenge, Zeus hides fire away from mankind but Prometheus discovered it and returned it back to mortals. Zeus punishes Prometheus once again by creating Pandora, and gave her to Prometheus' brother, Epimetheus (meaning "Hindsight") as a gift. Epimetheus married Pandora but Prometheus warned him not to. As a gift, the gods gave Pandora a jar (or a box, according to later sources) which she was told not to open. Curious about what was inside, Pandora opened it and out flew all the evil spirits and diseases to wreak havoc on the world. Pandora shut the jar, but the only one to stay inside was Hope.

Hesiod also tells of the myth where Zeus captures Prometheus and chains him to the Caucasus Mountains where an eagle descends to eat his liver each night. When the eagle leaves, the liver regrows and the eagle comes back the next night. Aeschylus portrays him in *Prometheus Unbound* as the preserver of mankind for helping them survive.

Cronus

Cronus, also known as Kronos, was the male personification of time which devours all things in the end. He was worshipped in Greece before the Hellenistic period but his worship wasn't as far spread as other original Greek deities.

Hesiod tells that Cronos was the son of Uranus and Gaea, the youngest out of all the Titans. His father imprisoned his brothers the Cyclops and the Hecatoncheires deep within the earth and so Gaea asked her youngest sons to help. Cronos and his four brothers devised a plan; when Uranus descended from the sky to lay with Gaea, the captured him, each holding a limb with Cronos in the middle as he castrated him. As a result, Cronos became the next ruler of the heavens and married his sister Rhea. Uranus prophesized that Cronos would be overthrown by his own offspring and so when Rhea gave birth to their children, Cronos devoured them all. However, on the advice of Gaea, Rhea was able to hide her youngest child, Zeus, in a mountain cave on the island of Crete and tricked her husband into swallowing a stone wrapped in swaddling clothes. Zeus grew to adulthood on Crete before he eventually overthrew his father, castrating him just as Cronos had done to his father. After his castration, Cronos was imprisoned deep within Tartarus but was eventually given kingship over Elysium.

Cronos ruled over the golden age of mankind according to Greek mythology but he was more widely worshipped by the Romans who identified him with Saturnus and was a principal agricultural deity. In art, Cronos was portrayed as an older man with a sickle or scimitar in hand.

Rhea

Rhea was one of the Titanides and the sister-wife of Cronos. She was widely worshipped throughout Greece, her worship pre-dating the Hellenistic period. She was the daughter of Uranus and Gaea and after her father's castration and imprisonment, married her younger brother. When she gave birth to their first five children, Cronos devoured them all in order to avoid a prophecy Uranus predicted. However, this angered Rhea and with the help of Gaea, she tricked her husband into swallowing a rock instead of their sixth child, and she was able to hide him away in a cave on Crete. Eventually, Zeus grew up and devised a plan that overthrew his father and forced him to expel his siblings.

Rhea's name translates as "flow" or "Ease", emphasizing her role as the female personification of the flow of time, the seasons. The flow was the flowing of menstrual blood, amniotic waters and breast milk. She was the goddess of motherhood, female fertility and comfort and was associated with Gaea and Cybele, the Great Mother of the Gods.

Themis

Themis was the Titan goddess of justice, wisdom and forethought, as well as being the explainer of divine will. In Hesiod's *Theogony*, Themis was the daughter of Uranus and Gaea but was occasionally identified with Gaea. She was the second wife of Zeus and by him she was the mother of the Horae, the Moirai and the Hesperides depending on the sources uses. On Mount Olympus, Themis' role was to keep border and oversaw ceremonies. In the *Eumenides* by Aeschylus she was the first owner of the oracle at Delphi but gifted it to her grandson Apollo. The worship of Themis was spread throughout the Greek world and was often depicted as a lovely woman with a pair of scales in her hand.

Chapter Four - Giants and Cyclops

In Greek mythology, the giants were known as the "earth-born". They were a race of oversized and many times, monstrous men born from Gaea and Uranus and related to the Olympian and Titan gods. Many of the giants feature in the Giant Wars, a battle between the gods and giants, but were ultimately defeated by Zeus and the younger gods.

Cyclops

The Cyclopes were a race of gigantic men with monstrous dispositions and are known for having only a single eye. Meaning "Round Eye", they were cannibals according to Homer, living as shepherds on an island which is often identified with Sicily. In Homers *Odyssey*, Odysseus meets with the Cyclops Polyphemus, who was a son of Poseidon, and eventually saved his men from being eaten by blinding him and escaping using the fleeces of Polyphemus' sheep. However, Hesiod claims that there were three Cyclopes who were the offspring of Gaea and Uranus who made Zeus' thunderbolts. Later writers claim that they worked for Hephaestus but were slain by Apollo as they crafter the thunderbolt which killed his son Asclepius.

Aloadae

The Aloadae were the twin sons of Iphimedia and Poseidon but was married to Aloeus at the time of the affair. They were called Otus and Ephialtes and grew up to be exceptionally strong and attempted to storm Mount Olympus; the myths tell that had Apollo not killed them before they grew to maturity, they would have defeated the gods. Another legend tells of how the Aloadae asked to marry the goddesses Artemis and Hera, the daughter and wife of Zeus respectively, Artemis transformed herself into a stag and darted in and about them. They each threw a spear at the deer but missed and killed the other.

Antaeus

Antaeus was a giant that lived in Libya and was a son of Gaea and Poseidon. When travelers passed through his lands they were required to wrestle with him; none survived the match. Hercules came to his lands and was requested to fight with him. However, no matter how many times Hercules threw him onto the ground, Antaeus grew stronger. Realizing that his strength came from the earth, Hercules grabbed Antaeus and lifted him off the earth before crushing him.

There are numerous ancient works of art which portray this famous myth but the earliest reference to the giant's strength originating from the earth comes from Ovid's *Metamorphoses* in Book IX.

Polyphemus

Polyphemus is one of the best known Cyclops in Greek mythology. Unlike the other Cyclopes, he was the son of Poseidon and the nymph Thoosa instead of being born to Gaea. Ovid tells how Polyphemus was enamored of the beautiful nymph Galatea, but she was in love with Acis. When he found out, Polyphemus grew angry and killed him. His most famous myth is found in *the Odyssey*, where the Greek hero Odysseus came to the island. Odysseus and his men were locked within Polyphemus' cave where he intended to eat them all. However, Odysseus managed to get the Cyclopes drunk and then drove a burning stake into his one eye when he had fallen asleep. When Polyphemus opened the cave to find help, Odysseus and his men used the fleece of his sheep, or clung to their bellies, to escape the cave. Polyphemus beseeched his father to avenge him and so Poseidon began his determination to thwart Odysseus' journey back home to Ithaca.

Typhon

Also known as Typhaon and Typhoeus, Typhon was the monstrous giant son of Gaea and Tartarus. Ancient writers portray him as a fearsome creature with 100 dragon heads who stormed Mount Olympus and drove the gods out of Greece. However, he was finally defeated by Zeus and thrown into the underworld. Another source claims that he was imprisoned in Cilicia or trapped under Mount Etna and his fiery temper caused volcanic eruptions. As such, Typhon was considered the male personification of volcanoes. He was married to Echidna, and together they created many of the monstrous creatures that feature in Greek mythology including Cerebus, the Hydra and the Chimera. His other offspring includes the typhoons.

Chapter Five – The Olympian Gods

The Olympian gods were the 12 great gods of the ancient Greeks, although others number them 13 as Dionysus replaced Hestia as an Olympian god. In actual fact, however, there were numerous Olympian gods but it is the 12 main gods which are typically referred to as 'Olympians'.

Zeus

Zeus is perhaps the best known of all the Greek gods. He was the ruler of the heavens, and the god of the sky and the weather. His weapons are the thunder and lightning bolts, and would send down the rain, the winds, lightning and thunder. There were three Zeus' worshipped throughout Greece, individual gods of the weather and forces of nature which ultimately were combined into one national deity.

According to mythology, Zeus was the youngest son of Cronos and Rhea. His other siblings had been swallowed whole by their father in order to escape the fate Cronos had inflicted on his own father. However, Rhea tricked her husband into swallowing a rock wrapped in swaddling clothes and safely hid the baby Zeus in a cave on the island of Crete. He was raised by the she-goat Amalthaea and protected by the Curetes who would bang their weapons loudly so that Zeus' crying couldn't be heard. When Zeus grew to adulthood, he devised a plan to overthrow his father. He was given a potion which he tricked Cronos into drinking, making him disgorge his brothers and sisters. Zeus and the younger gods rose up against the Titans, overthrowing them and castrating Cronos, before imprisoning them into the depths of the earth.

After this, Zeus and his brother, Poseidon and Hades, drew lots to determine who would rule over what part of the world. Zeus got the heavens, Poseidon the sea and Hades the underworld. Zeus then led the gods against the giants and also stopped numerous rebellions by other gods, including that of his third wife, Hera. He dwelled on Mount Olympus where he could look down upon the world so he could reward the good and punish those who committed crimes. Zeus was the father of the world, the protector of mankind, but he is mostly famous for the countless love affairs he had with goddesses and mortal women, producing a vast amount of divine, semi-divine and mortal children. Some of these unions were in the guise of animals – as a beautiful white bull in the case of Europa or a swan when he loved Leda – but sometimes they were conceived in more abstract forms such as a shower of gold. Although many believe he was married to just Hera, the queen of the gods, he was married twice before her, firstly to the Titan goddess Metis whom he swallowed when she was pregnant with Athena, and then to Themis.

Zeus was worshipped throughout Greece after the Hellenistic period came about and was the national deity, but local deities such as Athena and Hera had a great amount of importance, usually overshadowing him at times. Indeed, the earliest temple to Zeus in Athens was not erected until the latter part of the 6th century BCE and his temple located at Olympia dates well after Hera's temple was established.

Aphrodite

Aphrodite was the goddess of beauty and sexual love, also known as Venus to the Romans. Her name means "born of the sea foam", since the word *aphros* translates as "foam"; indeed, Hesiod tells that Aphrodite was born of the castrated genitals of Uranus that were thrown into the sea by Cronos. As such, Aphrodite could also be considered a younger Titan goddess, but she is more recognizable as an Olympian goddess. She was widely worshipped throughout the classical world as a sea goddess, a goddess of war (particularly at Sparta), but is more commonly known as the goddess of physical love, gracefulness, beauty and fertility. She was the patron goddess of prostitutes but her public cult was quite strict and serious.

The origin of Aphrodite's worship is believed to be from the Middle East region, with various characteristics and myths emphasizing this. Homer calls her Cyprian due to her worship on the island of Cyprus but by the time of Homer Aphrodite had been transformed into a Hellenistic deity and was called the daughter of Zeus and Dione.

Homer tells that Aphrodite was married to Hephaestus, the lame smith-god, but was not happy with him and embarked on a passionate love affair with Ares, the god of war. By Ares, she was the mother of Harmonia, Eros ad the twins Phobos and Deimos. Her love affair with Ares is one of her major myths; in it, Hephaestus learns that his wife is having an affair and so hatches a plan to catch them both in the act. Hephaestus creates an inescapable silver net and places it in her room. When Ares arrives to see Aphrodite, the net catches them both. Hephaestus invited all the other gods to laugh at Aphrodite and Ares before finally releasing them. Aphrodite and Hephaestus divorced and both went on to have other lovers.

Aphrodite had numerous love affairs with both gods and mortals. Her most famous mortal lovers included Anchises (becoming the mother of Aeneas) and Adonis.

Aphrodite was worshipped throughout the Greek world but her principal seats of worship were on Cyprus (which is where her cult is believed to have emerged first) and Corinth in Greece.

Apollo

In Greek mythology, Apollo was the son of Zeus and the Titan goddess Leto, and the twin brother of Artemis. Apollo had many functions in ancient Greek religion and was one of the most influential deities next to Zeus. His origins are shrouded in mystery; it is believed that his roots lay in Anatolia and then introduced to Egypt before arriving in Greece. By the time of Homer, Apollo had been transformed into a Hellenistic god, presiding over divine law and the establishment of cities, the god of prophecy and oracles, music, song, poetry, archery, disease, healing and looking after youngsters. In addition to this, he was a god of agriculture and herds, protecting herds from harm which can be seen from his epithet Alexikakos, meaning "Averter of Evil". Since his forename was Phoebus, meaning "bright", Apollo was seen to be a god of light and associated with the sun.

The myth surrounding his birth is one of his most recognizable stories. His mother was the Titan goddess Leto who was loved by Zeus. When his wife Hera found about the affair she sent a serpent to torment Leto and decreed anyone helping Leto would be punished. Fearing Hera's wrath, no one would help Leto until she made her way to the floating island of Delos. Here, she gave birth to Apollo (some myths claim that she gave birth to Artemis in a sacred grotto before reaching the island, with Artemis helping her mother give birth to Apollo). When Apollo was born, Delos grew pillars underneath, fixing itself to the earth.

Apollo was the god that presided over the oracle at Delphi, one of the most influential oracles in the ancient world. There are several myths which tell how he came about to preside over it. In one legend, his grandmother Themis was presiding over it but she gave it to him as a gift; another legend tells that after his birth he journeyed to Delphi where the dragon Python guarded the oracle and killed him. From there he transformed himself into a dolphin and jumped onto a Cretan ship and made them worship him. The cult of Apollo on Minoan Crete would go on to supersede that of the cult of Gaea that had already been established beforehand.

Apollo had many myths which concerned love affairs but most of these ended up disastrously. In one myth, he loved the nymph Daphne but she ran away from him and after begging to the other gods, was transformed into the laurel tree. Apollo gave the gift of prophecy to Cassandra but she spurned his advances and so was cursed that no one believed in.

Ares

Ares was the Greek god of war, but more specifically, the terrifying and bloody aspect of war. Despite the amount of wars and battles that raged across ancient Greek history, Ares was not a popular deity and there are few shrines and temples dedicated to him. However, during times of war people would perform religious rites to him.

Homer calls Ares the son of Zeus and Hera and was an Olympian god. From tracing the history of Ares, it appears that he originated in northern Greece, most likely in Thrace. He was offered both human and dog sacrifices at Sparta and was also worshipped in Colchis (modern day Georgia) where a dragon guarded the Golden Fleece.

According to mythology Ares was not popular with the rest of the gods, even by his parents. However, he still had many affairs with goddesses and mortal women. By Aphrodite he was the father of Phobos (Panic) and Deimos (Fear), Harmonia, Eros and Anteros; other children he sired include Nike, the Amazonian Warriors, Diomedes, Dryas, Lykos and Thrassa.

Ares was connected to several gods but usually in relation to his brutal warlike aspect. Indeed, his relationship with Aphrodite is an ancient one and at Sparta she was considered an early war goddess. He was accompanied in war by his sister, Eris (meaning "Strife") and his sons Phobos and Deimos.

Artemis

Known as the Mistress of the Hunt, Artemis was the goddess of childbirth, wild animals, hunting, vegetation and one of only a few virgin goddesses in the Greek pantheon. She was the daughter of Zeus and Leto, and often called the twin sister of Apollo. She was an extremely popular goddess in Greek society and worshipped throughout the country and beyond. Her roles vary from location to location, but ultimately she was the personification of the wild characteristic of the natural world.

The origin of her worship is most likely to lie on the island of Crete before the Hellenistic period. There were several myths which tell of her origins, making her the daughter of Zeus, Poseidon, Dionysus and Pallas, although the common version was that she was the daughter of Zeus and Leto. She appears as a local deity in several locations – Arcadia, Ephesus and Tauris – and eventually was merged into one national Hellenistic goddess. All three Artemis' were goddesses of wild nature, and she had several names in various locations. At Tauris, she was worshipped with human sacrifices in the earliest times; this was also the case at Sparta, until the sacrifices were replaced with the sprinkling of young boys' blood.

Artemis was widely regarded as the twin sister of Apollo. Some accounts claim that she was born earlier than her brother at Ortygia and later helped her mother give birth to Apollo. However, there is evidence that Apollo and Artemis were not siblings, but husband and wife in the earliest accounts, being the female counterpart of the god.

In pre-Homer poetry, writers told of fantastic, passionate love stories of the goddess' nymphs which appear to be of Artemis herself. However, after Homer, classical writers emphasized Artemis' chaste and virginal nature, focusing on her love for the hunt and dancing.

Athena

Also spelled Athene, Athena was the virgin goddess of war, wisdom, crafts and agriculture and the daughter of Zeus. In many ways, she was the opposite of the goddess Artemis and the god Ares, who were the wilder counterparts of her functions. There are two main versions of her conception and birth. In one, she was the daughter of Zeus and Metis, Zeus' first wife and the goddess of wisdom. Zeus learnt that any son born to Metis would be stronger than he and so Zeus swallowed Metis whilst she was pregnant. Eventually, Athena was born from Zeus' head. Another version was that Athena was conceived and born to Zeus without a mother.

It is most likely that Athena was pre-Hellenistic goddess who was later transformed into a national Greek deity. There was one version that makes Athena the daughter of Pallas, the winged giant from Libya, but looking closer at the myth shows that it is more likely that she was of Greek origin and her worship introduced to Libya where the myths took on several local elements before being reintroduced back into Greece. Other versions make her the daughter of the gods Poseidon and Triton. If we look at her as the daughter of Zeus, the all-powerful father of the gods, and Metis, the goddess of wisdom, Athena was a combination of the two – blending both power and wisdom. Ancient writers show her as an ethical character instead of the physical representation of a certain natural phenomenon.

In Homer's *The Iliad*, Athena was a goddess of war – more specifically, the goddess of wisdom and good counsel in war. She was the embodiment of the civilized aspect of war, a complete contrast to her brother Ares, the brutal aspect of battle and slaughter in war. In *The Iliad*, she fought on the side of the Greeks and was a skilled fighter, with Homer emphasizing her as an example of excellence in combat. She was the patron goddess of many heroes, including Odysseus on his way home after the Trojan War, as well as Perseus and Hercules in other myths.

Athena was a popular goddess throughout Greece and many acropolis, citadels and temples dedicated to her. Initially, she was worshipped in the palaces of local kings but after the Mycenaean period, the palaces were replaced by citadels. Athens was her cult centre where she was the patron deity. Myths tell of how she competed with the god Poseidon for control of the city. However, created the most useful object would have the city; Poseidon created the horse and brought forth a saltwater spring but Athena created the olive tree which gave the inhabitants food, wood and olive oil. Athena was awarded the city which was named Athens in her honour. This contest can be found on the Parthenon at the Acropolis, which is still a symbol of the great goddess.

Demeter

Demeter was the daughter of Cronos and Rhea, the sister of Zeus, and the goddess of agriculture. Her name is considered to be the same as ge meter, meaning Mother Earth, whereas others connect it with deo which originates from the Cretan word deai, meaning barley; as a result, this would indicate that Demeter was the Mother of Barley, or the giver of barley. Either way, the character and role of the goddess confirms her as an agricultural goddess.

Homer does not mention Demeter very often and is not classed as an Olympian deity but her roots most likely pre-date many of the Olympian gods. This can be seen in her most famous legend, the search for her daughter Persephone, who was snatched away by Hades who wanted her as his bride. For a long time, Demeter searched the world for Persephone, neglecting the fertility of the crops, causing a famine amongst mankind. Along the way, she established the Eleusinian Mysteries to the people of Eleusis who welcomed her. Eventually, she learnt that Zeus had given permission to Hades to wed Persephone and tried to persuade her to return to Olympus but Demeter refused. Zeus sent a messenger down to the underworld to bring Persephone back to Olympus but since she had eaten part of a pomegranate, it was decided that she stay with Hades for part of the year and the rest with her mother. This myth thus explained the changing of the seasons and why nothing grows during the winter.

Demeter was the goddess of agriculture but she was also the goddess of childbirth, health, marriage and an underworld deity. At Sparta, she was worshipped in this role in addition to the city of Argolis. She was worshipped at the festivals of Chthonia in Argolis, Haloa, Chloia, Proerosia, Thalysia, the Thesmophoria and the Skirophora. Many of these festivals celebrate her role as an agricultural divinity with sacrifices of baskets of flowers and grain.

Dionysus

Dionysus, who was known in Roman society as Bacchus or Liber Pater, was the son of Zeus and Semele and the god of wine, fruitfulness, vegetation and ecstasy. Dionysus is sometimes referred to as the 13th Olympian god due to the myth that Hestia gave up her role as one of the 12 great Olympian gods and gave it to Dionysus.

Dionysus was the son of Zeus. The god was having an affair with the beautiful princess, Semele, who was the daughter of King Cadmus of Thebes. Hera discovered the affair, disguised herself and convinced Semele to ask her lover to reveal his true form. When Zeus visited his pregnant mistress, she tried to get him to show himself; Zeus refused but eventually he gave in to her relentless pleas. He transformed himself into a lightning bolt which struck and killed her. Wanting to save the child, he cut the growing baby out of Semele and placed him into his thigh. When Dionysus was old enough, he emerged from Zeus, hence his name – "Twice Born". Baby Dionysus was given to the messenger god Hermes who then placed him in the care of the bacchantes (also known as the *thyiads* or the maenads of Mount Nysa. At various locations throughout Greece, he was said to have been raised by local nymphs. A Spartan myth tells that Semele and Dionysus were locked away in a chest and cast out to sea where the landed in Sparta, Semele dead but Dionysus alive.

It is still unclear as to the origins of Dionysus' worship. We have evidence in the form of his name inscribed on a clay tablet in the Linear B script, dating to around the 13th century BCE, long before the Mycenaean period. He is not mentioned as a great god by Homer, but instead as the deity who teaches mankind how to create wine. It is believed that his roots lie in Asia Minor (particularly from the Phrygian and Lydian regions) and gained much of his wild and dissolute character from being introduced into India before being worshipped in Greece.

Although this myth of being the son of Zeus is common knowledge for those who have read Greek mythology, there is deeper implication into his name "Twice Born". Early Orphic myths surrounding Orpheus tell that Zeus had a son called Zagreus by his own daughter, Persephone. When Hera found out about the infant, she had the baby cut into pieces, cooked and then devoured by the Titans. However, Athena was able to rescue the heart and was restored back to life through Semele, hence the name Dionysus, meaning "Twice Born". Zeus killed the Titans with a lightning bolt, their bodies turned to ashes. From these ashes were born the first-born humans.

Dionysus was much loved by the people and there were a number of festivals and celebrations held throughout the year in his honour. The Great Dionysia and the Lenaea festivals were held in Athens. As a god of fertility, the phallus made a regular appearance in his rites. There is evidence that he was offered human sacrifices in his early worship but was later substituted for animals, particularly the ram.

Hermes

Hermes was the son of Zeus and the goddess Maia, known as the messenger god as well as the god of thieves, cunning, gracefulness, animal husbandry, language, writing, astronomy, athletics and astrology. He was the messenger of Zeus, declaring the god's divine will. His name is most likely to originate from the Greek word for a group of stones which were used to show boundaries or landmarks.

He was said to have been born in a cave on Mount Cyllene in Arcadia, with the archaeological record indicating that the earliest cult of Apollo was established here. Here, Hermes was considered to be a fertility god and the depictions of the god show indecent images of the phallus to emphasize this role. The earliest temple dedicated to Hermes was in Arcadia, built by Lycaon, and then was introduced into Athens.

Hermes features in numerous myths, usually as the divine protector of sheep and cattle. In literature, he is connected with agricultural gods, especially that of nymphs and Pan. Homer tells that Apollo was the messenger of the gods and who would accompany the souls of the dead down to the underworld. In addition to these roles, other writers call him a god of dreams, and that humans would typically offer him the final libations before they went to bed. In his role as a messenger god, he is considered a god of roads, doorways and of travelers. He was also considered a god of music, having created the first lyre.

In art, Hermes was depicted as a handsome young man with golden blonde hair and "the first down upon his mouth". He typically wore a long tunic with a traveler's cap and winged boots. At times, he was shown carrying a sheep over his shoulders or holding the herald's staff (also known as the caduceus). However, by the 5th century BCE, Hermes was generally shown as a naked athlete.

Hestia

Hestia was a daughter of Cronos and Rhea, the sister of Zeus, and was swallowed by her father at the moment of her birth. In Greek mythology, she was the goddess of the hearth and one of the 12 great Olympian gods but later writers tell that she gave up her seat of power and gave it to Dionysus.

Hestia was one of only a few Greek goddesses who remained virgins. Both Poseidon and Apollo attempted to court her but she went to Zeus and swore an oath that she would forever remain a virgin. As a result, Zeus gave her a boon – that she would oversee all sacrifices made to the gods.

Hestia was worshipped mainly within the home as the goddess of the hearth. However, she was also worshipped by the entire town at the public civic hearth within the town hall. Since a town or a city was considered a family on a grander scale, she had great influence. Her fires in the public hearth were never allowed to go out and when towns sent groups of settlers out to colonize new areas, they would take a flaming torch lit at the public hearth. Hestia had a good relationship with Zeus due to their roles as familial divinities. When sacrifices were made to the gods in the home, Hestia took the first portion as goddess of the sacred hearth. In art, Hestia was depicted as a veiled goddess sometimes holding a flowering branch.

Hephaestus

Hephaestus was the lame smith-god and the god of fire. He was the son of Zeus and Hera, although other versions claim that Hera conceived him without Zeus' help since she was jealous of Zeus siring Athena by himself. It appears that Hephaestus' origins lay in Asia Minor as with many of the Greek gods but was soon Hellenised.

Hephaestus was lame as he was thrown out of the heavens twice; the first time by Hera who was disgusted at the sight of him and then later by Zeus after he dared stand on his mother's side against Zeus. Homer tells that he was married to Charis in *The Iliad*, but in *the Odyssey*, Homer tells that he was married to Aphrodite. However, Aphrodite was not faithful to him and he humiliated her and her lover, Ares, in front of all the gods when he trapped them within a silver net.

He appears to be the male equivalent to that of Athena in that he shared his knowledge of craftsmanship – especially that of metalworking – to mankind, yet was still regarded as inferior to the goddess. He had a workshop on Mount Olympus but later writers transfer it to a volcano, with the natural volcanic forces being attributed to him. Hephaestus was not as widely worshipped as other Greek gods, his cult arrived in Athens around 600 BCE and his other main cult centre was located on the island of Lemnos.

Poseidon

Poseidon was the son of Cronos and Rhea, and the brother of Zeus and Hades, and the husband of the sea goddess Amphitrite. In Greek mythology, Poseidon was the god of the sea, of earthquakes and horses. He is often mistaken for Pontus, the personification of the sea itself and the eldest of the water or sea gods.

When he was born, he was swallowed whole by his father but subsequently released when Zeus made their father disgorge them. After the Titan War, the brothers drew lots to determine who would rule over the heavens, the sea and the underworld. Poseidon became the ruler of the oceans. His main symbol was that of the trident, which may have initially have been a fish spear which transformed into the trident over a period of time.

Even though Poseidon was the god of the sea, he was also the god of earthquakes and dry land. Some of the god's earliest cult centres were actually deep inland where was called *"enosichthon"*, meaning *earth-shaker*. He was also the god of horses, and it is believed that he was introduced by the Hellens as they brought the first horses into Greece around the second century BCE. Indeed, many of Poseidon's offspring includes horses, the most famous being that of Pegasus by the Gorgon Medusa.

Poseidon was the husband of Amphitrite but like many male gods, had many affairs with goddesses and mortal women. Many of his sons become the founders of towns and cities throughout the country in addition to siring the Cyclops, the monstrous human-eating one-eyed giants.

Hera

Known as the Queen of the Heavens, Hera was the sister-wife of Zeus and the mother of Hephaestus, Ares and Eileithyia. She was the goddess of marriage and childbirth and the patron goddess of Argos. She was the third wife of Zeus but she is well-known for her relentless hounding and punishments of Zeus' lovers and offspring.

Hera was worshipped throughout Greece, particularly at Argos, Samos and Athens. In Argos, her festivals were mainly agricultural in nature but she also had one referred to as The Shield, and an armored marched procession on Samos. These kinds of festivals emphases her role as the queen of the heavens since a city goddess must be able to rule in both times of war and in during peaceful periods.

Chapter Six - Other Important Gods

There are thousands of deities in the Greek pantheon, many of which are considered Olympian gods. These include the god Hades, ruler of the underworld. He was one of the three sons of Cronos and the brother of Zeus. Although not one of the 12 great Olympic gods, he was still an important Olympian god nonetheless.

Hades

Hades was the brother of Zeus and Poseidon, and the ruler of the underworld, the place where the souls of the dead go after they have finished their mortal lives. He is most famous for the abduction of his niece, Persephone, whom he married. He was sometimes referred to as the chthonian Zeus, meaning the underworld Zeus, emphasizing his role as ruler of the land of the dead.

Amphitrite

Amphitrite was the goddess of the seas and the wife of Poseidon. She was one of the Nereids, the 50 daughters of Nereus and Doris, making her the granddaughter of Pontus, the earliest Greek sea god. She is well-known for fleeing from Poseidon when he tried to court her, but was eventually persuaded to accept his proposal by Delphinus.

Asclepius

Asclepius was the son of Apollo and the mortal princess Coronis and later deified as the god of healing. He was taught medicine by the wise centaur Chiron and Zeus, scared that Asclepius would heal all mortals and not allow them to die, struck him with a thunderbolt. In revenge, Apollo killed the Cyclopes who created the thunderbolt. Homer refers to him as an excellent physician in *the Iliad* but later writers call him a hero and ultimately a god. His worship started in Thessaly but soon found its way all over the country and by 293 BCE, established at Rome.

Cabeiri

The Cabeiri, also known as the Cabiri, the Kabeiroi and Kabiri, was a group of divinities of Pelasgian origins but spread throughout Greece, particularly at Macedonia, central Greece and Asia Minor. These divinities are shrouded in mystery and were fertility gods and watched over seafarers. In the earliest time of their worship, there were numerous deities but by the classical period, there were only two male gods, Axiocersus and his son and assistant Cadmilus, and two female divinities called Axierus and Axiocersa, all of which were associated with other gods from the national Greek pantheon. They were often identified with the Samothracian gods whose mystery cult has long been of interest.

Chapter Seven - Hercules

Of all the famous Greek heroes, there are none whose courageous acts and outstanding endeavors were more praised than Hercules. The son of Zeus and Alcmene, Hercules has become the center character of numerous myths and legends of the ancient Greece.

According to the story, Alcmene, fearing the wrath of Hera, who did not look kindly on her husband's constant affairs, entrusted Hercules to one of her faithful servant's right after he was born. Alcmene hoped that in this way she could protect the child from the vengeful goddess.

The servant, following her instructions, left the child out in the field, confident that no harm would come to the son of Zeus. Not long after, Athena and Hera came across the child and took pity on him. At Athena's suggestion, Hera took baby Hercules to her breasts to feed him, but the child was so strong that he was causing her immense pain. Infuriated, Hera dropped Hercules to the ground and left.

Athena, however, felt sorry for the baby and took him to Alcmene's house which was nearby. Not knowing she was his mother, Athena entrusted Alcmene with the child, and she was naturally all too happy to take her child back, with none being the wiser about his true origins. And so, blessed by gods from his very first breath, young Hercules found his way back home.

Strangling the snakes

Hera, as vengeful and spiteful as she was, didn't take long to put two and two together. Realizing whom she helped caused her to be filled with rage, she sent two snakes to Hercules' cradle to kill him. When Alcmene heard her child crying in the other room, she rushed in, only to find that Hercules had strangled the snakes all on his own.

Alcmene's husband Amphitryon, who was clueless about the baby's origin, was shocked by what he saw and immediately consulted Tiresias, a well-known seer, about what kind of sign it was. Tiresias revealed to him the divine origins of the child, announcing an illustrious future for young Hercules.

Hercules' childhood and youth

Upon discovering the great destiny awaiting his stepson, Amphitryon set out to give the child the best possible education and upbringing. Young Hercules was taught to handle the bow and ride the chariot among other things.

But from the very young age, Hercules displayed a rash and intolerable nature. He didn't take criticism all too well, and once his bow teacher tried to use blows to correct his mistakes, he killed the tutor on the spot.

As the hero grew, his extraordinary stature and great strength became more prominent. His peers both admired and feared him. Talented in many things, he quickly became masterful in handling the bow and arrow, lance and spear. But, his physical development did not tame his temper. Always prone to rash reactions, often with fatal consequences, young Hercules caused his parents many headaches.

As he came to be of age, it was time for the young hero to make some choices about his future life. Olympian gods blessed him with great strength and many talents, but he alone had to decide how these talents would be used. And so, Hercules removed himself from the world to spend some time in solitude and meditation, trying to discern the hidden divine design.

As Hercules meditated deep in the forest, two beautiful female creatures visited him. They were Virtue and Vice. Vice was very attractive and filled with numerous earthly desires and sins. Virtue was noble and pure as she stood for high ideals and moral values of the Greek world.

Both females were there to try and seduce the son of Zeus. Each of them wanted to attract Hercules to take her path and he had to make a difficult choice. Vice promised him the life of pleasure, riches and luxury. She tempted Hercules with promises of great earthly pleasures requiring no efforts on his part.

Virtue spoke to him about the path less attractive but nobler. She promised him that good things would come his way if he put in the required effort and lived his life in a respectful manner, following his conscience. Gods see your efforts Virtue told Hercules and will reward you accordingly.

Upon careful reflection, being the hero that he was, Hercules naturally opted for the path of virtue. He promised to devote his life to respecting the will of the gods and serving his country to the best of his abilities.

First great deeds

Making his choices, Hercules returned home to Mount Cithaeron, ready to perform great deeds in honor of gods and to the service of his fellow countrymen. He wouldn't have to wait long to prove himself as the first challenge awaited him as soon as he returned.

Upon his arrival, Hercules was informed that a ferocious lion set up his lair near the village and was creating fear and havoc among the local people, killing their herds and terrorizing the shepherds. The son of Zeus would have none of that, and he immediately went in the mountains to confront the lion. When he spotted him wandering, Hercules immediately rushed at the beast and struck a deadly blow with his sword. Afterward, he skinned the animal and used its hide to create a cape and helmet for himself. This is why Hercules is usually depicted with a lion's hide on his back.

Returning home from his very first task, Hercules encountered Minyan envoys on their way to Thebes to collect the annual tribute. Theban by birth and by the hearth, Hercules was deeply insulted by the injustice and humiliation inflicted upon his hometown. Once again, his rash temper took over and he proceeded to mutilate the envoys, sending them back to their king Erginus.

Erginus, as any king would be, was infuriated by this treatment of his messengers and gathered an army to attack Thebes unless they agreed to surrender Hercules to him. Theban king Creon was ready to comply with the Erginus' demand, fearing his wrath but once again Hercules demonstrated his courage.

He gathered a group of young and fearless Theban men and advanced against Erginus' army. They successfully defeated much greater Minyan army but during the confrontation, Amphitryon, Hercules' stepfather, and tutor, lost his life. Further enraged by this, Theban hero proceeded with his small but selected army to the gates of Orchomenus, the Minyan capital. Hercules mastered a great victory over his enemies and proceeded to burn the city to the ground. When he returned to Thebes, he was celebrated as a great hero. King Creon gave him his daughter's hand and numerous gods honored his courage with their gifts. From goddess Athenes he received a leather coat, the divine blacksmith Hermes gave him a sword, Apollo sent him special arrows, while Hephaestus honored him with a golden quiver.

Twelve tasks of Hercules

Probably the most famous myth about Hercules is the one depicting his twelve great tasks. Everyone even remotely interested in Greek mythology has heard of at least a few of these tasks. But how did it come about for the hero of Thebes to undertake this perilous path?

Just before Hercules was to be born, Zeus made an announcement to the rest of the Olympian gods that the one who was to be born on that day, the grandson of Perseus, would rule all men. Hera immediately figured out that her husband was talking about Hercules, the son he made with Alcmene. To put a wedge in the prophecy, Hera solicited the help of goddess Eileithyia to postpone the birth of Hercules. Then she gave birth to her son, Eurystheus, who was also the grandson of Perseus, on that day, making him, by the will of Zeus, the ruler of all men.

Thus, even mighty Hercules had to subject to his will. Once the word of his brave deeds started spreading through the world, Eurystheus became jealous of his natural rival and decided to get rid of him by sending him on the series of deadly tasks. Eurystheus was hoping that Hercules would be killed during one of these tasks, and thus, he would keep his hands clean and remove his adversary.

As expected, Hercules did not take the orders well. Rebellious in nature, the Theban hero felt humiliated and was ready to refuse the orders and stand up to Eurystheus. However, before he made his decision public, Zeus appeared to Hercules and advised him not to go against his destiny but to embrace it instead. Receiving the word from his father, he finally complied and consulted the Delphi oracle about what was awaiting him. There he was told that once he had finished ten tasks for Eurystheus, he would be free once again.

Although Hercules accepted his destiny, he wasn't happy about it and he started to feel down and depressed. His eternal enemy,

Hera used the moment of weakness and further influenced the hero to completely darken his mind. In this state of complete madness, Hercules proceeded to kill his own children. When he finally got better, Hercules realized the severity of what he had done and decided the only way he could feel better about himself was to take on Eurystheus' tasks without any further delay.

1. The Nemean Lion

The Nemean lion was a horrible beast that was pillaging the area between Cleone and Nemea and no one was brave enough to stand against it. Eurystheus, hoping that the lion would mark the end of Hercules, sent him to kill the beast and bring him its hide as the proof.

Hercules had no problems finding the lion but killing it proved to be a difficult task indeed. His arrows could not damage the animal's skin and it became clear that his weapons were useless. So, Hercules snuck upon the beast, hit it on the head with his club and using the short moment of confusion grabbed it by its neck and strangled it to death.

Then he proceeded to make a new armor for himself from the Nemean lion's skin and thus attired, appeared before Eurystheus. He was terrified of what Hercules might do to him, knowing of his short fuse so sent his messenger Copreus to deal with him instead.

2. Slaying the Hydra

Since Hercules survived his first task, Eurystheus now sent him to face the dreaded Hydra, a nine-headed serpent-like monster, which sowed fear among the people of Lerna. One of Hydra's heads was immortal so Eurystheus was convinced that this time Hercules would certainly fail.

Upon arriving at Lerna, Hercules first used his arrows to force the Hydra to get out of her lair. Then he chased her into the woods and proceeded to hit her fiercely with his club. However, as soon as he managed to chop off one of her heads, two new ones appeared.

Seeing his tactics not working, Hercules took a new approach and had his cousin Iolaus, who accompanied him to Lerna, set fire to the nearby trees. He then used burning branches to sear the necks of the monster as soon as he chopped off her heads, preventing new ones from growing out.

When he finally got rid of all the other heads, Hercules chopped off the immortal one, and since it could not be killed, he buried it in the ground and rolled a big stone over it so no one would ever find it.

He also used the monster's poisonous blood, dipping his arrows in it, making them even more deadly than before.

3. Capturing the Horned Hind

Next on the list of Hercules' tasks were capturing the horned hind Cerunitis. The sacred animal of Artemis proved to be hard to catch without hurting it. In the end, he had to wound it with one of his arrows.

Once he subdued the animal, which had golden antlers and brass hoofs, he took it on his back and started his journey back to Eurystheus, after a whole year spent in pursue. On his way back, he ran into Artemis, who was at first very upset that Hercules had hurt her favorite animal but eventually relented and let him continued his journey.

4. Subduing the Erymanthian Boar

There was a fierce boar, pillaging the Erymanthian region. No one else being a match for the animal, Hercules was tasked with subduing the beast and bringing it back to Eurystheus alive.

During his journey to find and capture the boar, one of the most famous episodes of Greek mythology happened, as Hercules met the Centaurs, mythical creatures with their upper part of the body human and lower part being that of a horse.

The Centaur named Pholus offered the son of Zeus food and shelter and Hercules gratefully accepted. However, he got an appetite for the Centaurs' famous wine and managed to convince Pholus to let him taste some.

As soon as a cask was open, a strong smell spread through the mountains, attracting other Centaurs, who did not take it kindly that the wine, which was a common property of all Centaurs, was served without their presence. They attacked the cave where Hercules was resting but were met with the kind of resistance they did not expect. The Theban hero drove them away and then proceeded to shoot them with his venomous arrows.

In the heat of battle, Hercules wounded a Centaur named Chiron, whom he befriended in the past. Hydras' blood proved a serious threat to Centaurs, who were immortal creatures and caused Chiron an agony, unlike anything he experienced ever before. In the end, he pleaded to the gods to grant him death despite his immortality just to end his sufferings. In a similar fashion, Hercules' host Pholus had fallen victim to his poisonous arrows.

The death of his friends caused Hercules a lot of grief and infuriated him; he continued with his task after giving Pholus a proper burial. When he finally encountered the boar, Hercules chased the animal all over the mountains until it finally had no energy left to keep running. He proceeded to tie up the boar and took him back to Mycenae.

5. Cleaning Augeas' Stables

The king Augeas of Elis was famous for his huge herds. According to the myth, there were three thousand cattle which resided near the palace and for a period of several years, nobody cleaned their stables.

Eurystheus tasked Hercules with this duty and obeying wishes of his father, the Theban hero complied, despite feeling degraded by such a task. He presented himself to king Augeas and told him he could clean his stables within one day but only if the king agreed to give him one tenth of the cattle.

Thinking this was impossible, Augeas agreed. Hercules combined his cunningness and his strength and redirected the water from two nearby rivers to flow through the stables, washing away all the refuse.

When the king of Elis saw Hercules did as promised, finding out this was a task given to him by Eurystheus, he refused to keep up his end of the bargain. Hercules brought the matter to the court, but Augeas banished both him and his (king's) son, who witnessed the promise, from his realm.

6. Chasing away the Stymphalides

The next task given to Hercules was to get rid of the Stymphalides, enormous birds of prey who shot sharp feathers from their wings. Upon arriving in Arcadia, Hercules tracked down a large flock of these birds but was uncertain on how best go about attacking them.

As he was thinking, goddess Athena, who always favored the hero, appeared to him and handed him brazen clappers made by Hephaestus. The noise this instrument produced was intolerable to the birds' hearing, and they started up in the air, flying around frantically. At this point, Hercules took out his bow and one by one; he killed most of them. Those that survived left the area, never to be seen again.

7. Capturing the Cretan Bull

This mythical task is connected to the famed Minos, the king of Crete. Namely, Minos vowed to Poseidon, the sea god; he would sacrifice to him the first animal that appeared out of the sea. To test his sincerity and devotion, Poseidon created a magnificent bull that appeared before the king's eyes. Charmed by its features, Minos took the animal for himself, sacrificing another animal instead.

Greek gods have never been known for their mercifulness or kindness and Poseidon, seeing Minos break his word, was enraged and caused the bull to lose his mind, and he started creating havoc all over Crete.

Since no one could subdue the bull, the king gladly gave his permission to Hercules to try. As expected, he not only captured the animal but actually tamed it to such a degree that he was able to ride it across the sea back to Mycenae. When the animal was delivered to him, Eurystheus set it free and the bull once again went mad and continued to cause trouble all over Greece until Theseus finally put an end to it, killing the bull on the Marathon fields.

8. Diomedes' Mares

Diomedes, the king of Bistonians, had a herd of large wild horses that preferred eating human flesh to grazing grass. To provide food for his horses, the king captured unwitting strangers who happened to enter his realm and threw them to the beasts.

Brave Hercules, sent to capture the mares, first caught Diomedes himself and threw him to his horses. As soon as the mares tasted the flesh of their master, they became tame, and Hercules had no problems bringing the herd back to the shore with him. However, the Bistonians launched a ferocious attack against their king's killer.

Hercules faced his attackers, entrusting his friend Abdures to take care of the mares. The hero made quick work of the Bistonians but when he returned from the battle, he discovered that the mares went mad once again and tore his friend to pieces.

Deeply saddened once again, Hercules buried his friend, built a town in his honor and then delivered the mares to Eurystheus who brought them to Mount Olympus to serve as food for wild beasts.

9. Capturing Hippolyte's Girdle

Hippolyte was the queen of the Amazons tribe, courageous warrior women, skilled in different aspects of the art of war. The queen was of divine origin herself, as her father was none other than Ares, the god of war. Ares gave Hippolyte a girdle of exquisite beauty, and she always wore it as a symbol of her power. It was this girdle that Hercules was tasked with acquiring and bringing to Eurystheus.

The hero of Thebes knew that this would be one of the hardest tasks he would have to face, as Amazons were known as fierce and fearless warriors. So, Hercules gathered a small but selected group of companions and embarked on the journey to Amazon.

Although they expected a lot of resistance, Hippolyte was so impressed by Hercules and the stories that were told about him that she agreed to give him the girdle as a present. The hero was about to complete one of his tasks without any hardships for the first time but once again envious Hera mixed her fingers in the matter.

Hera took a form of an Amazon and started spreading rumors that Hercules and his friends were there to kidnap their queen. Always ready to do battle, it didn't take more than a rumor for the Amazons to take to arms and attack Hercules and his friends. Many warriors fell or were injured on the battlefield, but Hercules eventually prevailed and received the girdle in exchange for Melanippe, one of the bravest Amazon warriors whom he was able to capture.

10. Capturing Geryon's Oxen

Hercules was now close to fulfilling the prophecy or at least he thought so, as he was sent to bring the oxen belonging to a giant Geryon. The terrifying giant had three bodies, with six hands, six legs and three heads.

Eurystheus had hoped that his would finally mark the end of Hercules as Geryon's cattle were protected by another giant, Gadria, as well as a two-headed dog Orthrus. But the ruler of men has once again underestimated the courage and strength of his cousin.

It was during this journey that Theban hero erected famous "Pillars of Hercules" in Africa. He then proceeded to threaten the Sun god Helios, who, struck by his courage, gave him a golden boat which brought him safely across the sea.

When Hercules landed in Erythia, he was immediately attacked. In another display of courage and super-human strength, he killed the guards and collected the animals. Then he proceeded to take them to the sea and had the herd swim across the sea and presented them to Eurystheus.

The hero expected this would mark an end of his servitude as the Delphi oracle told him he would only have to perform ten tasks. However, Eurystheus told him that he wouldn't count the Hydra or clean the stables because in the first instance he had help and in the other he tried to get paid for his work. And so, Hercules had to agree to do two more tasks before he would be free of his pledge.

11. Hesperides' Apples

Goddess Gaea presented Hera with a magic tree that produced golden apples. The tree was guarded at all times by Hesperides, daughters of Night and a hundred-headed dragon. But all these troubles were not the worst Hercules had to endure in this task, as he had no idea about the location of the garden where the tree was located so he had to spend a lot of time to find the location.

During his journey, Hercules experienced many adventures, facing even the god of war, Ares himself, after he killed his son in a duel. Ares and Hercules fought for a long time, and the battle would have lasted for who knows how long if Zeus didn't get involved and put a stop to the battle.

He then continued his quest and captured Nereus, the old sea god and the only being who knew the whereabouts of the Hesperides' garden. After he had managed to defeat him, Hercules forced Nereus to tell him the location.

Continuing on his path, our hero came across bound Prometheus and killed the vicious eagle that came every night to peck his liver and set him free. Grateful Prometheus gave further instructions to Hercules on how to find the apples. He told him that the garden was near the place where Atlas supported the heavens on his shoulders and further instructed Hercules that instead of trying to get the apples himself, he should send Atlas for them and take his place as the holder of heavens during his absence.

Atlas gladly accepted Hercules' suggestion and successfully procured the apples. But, when he returned, he refused to once again take his place and told the hero he would take the apples to Eurystheus himself and live the life of freedom. Hercules, quickly realizing his unpleasant situation, pretended to accept his fate and asked Atlas to only take the heavens on his shoulders for a brief moment so he could make a pad for his head. Once Atlas agreed and relieved Hercules of his burden, he thanked him, picked up the apples and went on his way back.

12. Capturing Cerberus

Since Hercules accomplished all other tasks, Eurystheus sent him to the final mission to go to the underworld and bring back the three-headed dog Cerberus. Eurystheus had hoped that Hercules' strength and might would be of no use to him in the realm of Hades.

Descending to the underworld, Hercules encountered bound Theseus and set him free. At the gates of the underworld, Hercules encountered the god of death Hades, who wouldn't let him pass. The hero shot him with one of his poisoned arrows, and the god felt the pain and suffering, unlike anything he experienced before. The agony changed Hades' opinion, and he allowed Hercules to enter but took all his weapons away, leaving him only his lion's skin and the armor.

Even without his weapons, Hercules was able to subdue Cerberus, grabbing the beast by its legs and throat and brought it back to the surface. Eurystheus, seeing that his plan to get rid of his rival failed once again returned Cerberus to Hercules, who gave it back to its rightful owner Hades.

Death of Hercules

After he was liberated from his servitude, Hercules undertook many more adventures, which even saw him become a slave to Omphale, queen of Lydia for a period of three years. However, finding out about his great deeds, the queen gave him his freedom and offered her hand and her kingdom.

After returning from Lydia, Hercules got married to Deianeira, the marriage which would prove to be his undoing. Although their marital life was at first happy, during one of many feasts, Deianeira's father accidently killed a young noble. For this accidental crime, Hercules banished him from the kingdom.

After that, he went with his wife and son to visit his friend King Ceyx. On the way there, he had to kill the Centaur Nessus, who tried to kidnap Deianeira. Hercules shot the Centaur with his poisoned arrow and Nessus, longing vengeance, tricked Deinaeira to catch some blood from his wound and store it away. The Centaur told her that should she ever feel that she was losing her husband's affection, she should use the blood to win him back.

Hercules' wife had no idea of the Centaur's evil plan and did as he told her, not telling her husband anything. Not long after, Hercules set out for what was going to be his last successful mission.

Upon conquering the city of Echalia, Hercules was on his way back and stopped to offer a sacrifice to Zeus. He sent for his sacrificial robe to be brought from Trachin. Deinaeira, fearing she was losing her husband's love, applied the Centaur's blood to the robe before sending it to Hercules.

The unsuspecting hero put on the robe and approached the fire to offer his sacrifice. The heat from the fire heated up the venom, and it entered his blood, causing him terrible agony. Hercules couldn't remove the robe as it was glued to his body and he realized that there was nothing he could do.

Hercules returned home, and when Deinaeira saw what she did, she was so sad and broken that she hanged herself. Hercules, upon giving his last wishes, ordered for a large pyre to be set up and set on fire so he could end his agony. When flames started going high into the air, the goddess Athena descended from the heavens, picked Hercules up in her chariot and took him to Mount Olympus to join the immortals.

This was the end of the hero's day in the world of men.

Chapter Eight - Jason And The Argonauts

Another well known Greek legend is that of Jason and the Argonauts and the quest for the Golden Fleece. Unlike Hercules, however, not many people actually know details of this interesting story.

Jason was the son of king Aeson, who had to abandon his realm when his younger brother Pelias decided to steal the throne. Jason spent ten years in the cave of the Centaur Chiron, who trained him in different arts and combat skills. But, as he grew older, the desire started growing for him to reclaim what was rightfully his. Eventually, he left the safety of the cave and set on the path to Iolcus to ask from Pelias to return the throne.

On his journey, Jason encountered goddess Hera, masked as an old woman seeking help. After giving it some thought, Jason decided to offer his assistance. For this, Hera was very grateful and showed to him in all her beauty, telling him who she was and promising him her protection for the rest of his life.

This gave Jason new wings, and when he arrived in Iolcus, he encountered Pelias at the marketplace, offering a sacrifice to Poseidon. When Pelias saw Jason, who was missing a sandal on his foot (which he lost helping Hera), he immediately remembered a prophecy which told that he would lose his kingdom to a man wearing just one sandal.

However, the king decided to hide his fear and welcomed his nephew, organizing feasts and celebrations in his honor for five days. On the sixth day, Jason requested the throne and the king, hiding his true intentions, said he would gladly accept his demand if he first went on an expedition for him. He explained that he had a vision in which Phryxus asked him to bring from Colchis his remains and the Golden Fleece, but he was too old to go himself.

Phyrxus was the son of the nymph Nephele and the human king Athamas. When Athamas divorced Nephele and married Ino, the nymph had to save her children from the wicked stepmother who wished them ill. She sent them far away on the back of a ram with Golden Fleece.

Phyrxus sister Helle did not survive the trip, but he arrived safely to Colchis. The king there welcomed him and even gave him the hand of one of his daughters. Thankful for his salvation, Phyrxus sacrificed the ram to Zeus and presented king Aetes with the Golden Fleece. The king, hearing the prophecy that his life was closely related to the safety of the fleece, placed it in a groove guarded by a large, always alert dragon.

Preparing the expedition

So, this was the fleece that Jason was tasked with taking. He was well aware that this would be a very difficult mission and decided to call upon the help of many heroes whom he befriended while he was living with Chiron. As usual, all heroes welcomed the invitation, always seeking a new chance to prove their valor.

Once he gathered his party, Jason turned to Argos, one of the best ship builders alive. Guided by Athena, Argos produced a large, beautiful ship for Jason and his crew and it was named Argo. The ship was so strong and sturdy that powers of wind and water could bring no harm to it. At the same time, it was so light that they could carry it around on land. With their ship done, the Argonauts, called this way after their ship was ready.

In total, there were fifty heroes on board Argos. Some of them included renown Hercules, Peleus, the father of Achilles, Theseus, later king of Athens, Ephemus, the son of Poseidon, Apollo's son Idmon the Seer and many others. Jason offered a sacrifice to Poseidon before embarking on the journey, and they started out on their brave and difficult expedition.

First adventures

The voyage was long, and the Argonauts were sure to meet many troubles along their way. Their first adventure happened when bad weather forced them to steer out of their way and take refuge on the island of Lemnos.

This island was populated by women only. The previous year, these women went mad with jealousy and murdered all men who lived there. Always prepared for battle, they noticed Argo approaching and armed themselves.

Heroes on Argo were stunned by what they were witnessing and sent out the message they were coming in peace. The queen of Lemnos Hypsipyle was at first reluctant to let them set foot on the land but changed her mind after an old nurse told her this was a great opportunity for them to procure some noble husbands who would protect them in times of distress.

Eventually, the Argonauts were allowed to come onto the island, and when Hypsipyle saw Jason, she was so charmed by his looks that she offered him to rule Lemnos. Jason accepted, and they spent a long time on the island, almost forgetting the goal of their expedition. In the end, Hercules, who was one of the few who decided to stay on the ship, came to the land and reminded them of their task.

As if awoken from their slumber by the words of Hercules, the Argonauts continued their quest and the voyage eventually led them to an island inhabited by Doliones, Poseidon's descendants. The Argonauts were welcomed by them and their king Cyzicus.

Most of the crew disembarked to attend the feast that the king arranged for them but Hercules, true to the form, stayed behind to guard the ship. All of a sudden a tribe of Giants, that were enemies of Doliones, started attacking the ship with huge rocks.

Hercules was able to eliminate a number of them using his poisoned arrows, and when other Argonauts became aware of what was going on, they rushed to help the Theban hero and killed the remainder of the Giants.

Defeating the Giants and ridding Doliones of their mortal enemies, the Argonauts once again set sail. However, bad weather forced them to look for shelter on an island once again. Unfortunately, since it was night, the inhabitants did not recognize their friends and a combat ensued, resulting in king Cyzicus' death. Only when the sun shed its light upon the earth did both parties realize what had happened and they spent three days lamenting the unfortunate events and the king's death.

Hercules leaves the band

When the lamentation period was over, the Argonauts continued their voyage, which led them to Mysia. Once again, the domestic population welcomed famous heroes, honoring them and organizing feasts and banquets.

Hercules once again decided he wouldn't partake. Instead, he went into the woods to look for a fir-tree. His adopted son Hylas went after him, and as he went through the forest, a nymph set her eyes upon him. Stunned by Hylas' beauty, she grabbed him and pulled him deep inside the fountain in which she resided. Polyphemus, who also happened to be in the forest, saw the whole thing and told Hercules about it. Two heroes set out to look for Hylas and Argo, carrying the rest of the band, left without them.

Once they realized Hercules wasn't among them, some Argonauts wanted to go back and get him, while others wanted to continue their journey. Their dispute was ended by the sea god Glaucus who told them that Hercules was left behind because it was Zeus' wish and that there was a different design awaiting him.

Further adventures

Continuing without Polyphemus and Hercules, the Argonauts next landed in the country of the Bebrycians. These people and their king had a custom that no stranger could leave their land before he matched his strengths with the king. The king Amycus then dueled with Pollux, who, after a long struggle, was able to defeat him and ended up killing him.

Free to leave, the Argonauts now ended up in Bithynia, governed by the blind king Phineus. Phineus was blinded by gods because he abused the gift of prophecy that was given to him. In addition, gods sent the Harpies to prevent him from enjoying the food, making his life completely miserable.

When Argonauts heard of his torments, they took pity on him and decided to help him. Two heroes, Zetes and Calais, defeated the Harpies and chased them away. Now at least Phineus was able to eat at peace and as a sign of his gratitude, using his gift to see the future, he revealed to the Argonauts many things that were awaiting them.

Jason and the Argonauts spent some days in the company of the king and then continued their voyage. After a short sail, they came upon two rocky islands, the Symplegades, which met and separated all the time. The only way forward was between these two rocks and Phineus' helped proved invaluable for this challenge. The blind king had instructed the Argonauts before they left to release a dove from their ship. If they see the dove pass between the islands, then the passage is safe. They did so and followed the dove, rowing the boat as fiercely as they could and arrived safely to the other side.

After passing between the islands, the Argonauts encountered the Stymphalides, which were only later chased away by Hercules. They managed to protect themselves from the birds' sharp feathers using their shields and helmets, leaving another danger behind. They also picked up four young men from a shipwreck, who were Jason's cousins and who shared with them more information about their final destination and the Golden Fleece.

The Argonauts reach Colchis

Soon after the incident with the Stymphalides, the Argonauts reached their final destination, the kingdom of Colchis. Upon anchoring the ship, they noticed the Golden Fleece glittering in the sacred grove of Ares.

The heroes held a council and decided that before they apply any more drastic measures, they should first try diplomacy and friendly approach. They wanted to explain their reasons for being there and ask the king Aetes to help them willingly. And so, Jason, with a few selected men, set out to meet with the king and explain their mission.

Jason's company included four sons of Phryxus and this news quickly spread through the palace. The king greeted his guests kindly and invited them to a feast prepared in their honor. But, when Jason finally revealed the reasons for his voyage, the king wouldn't hear any of it, claiming that the Fleece was rightfully his. Wanting to avoid the bloodshed at all costs, Jason tried to appease Aetes and asked him to assign them with a task which would prove them worthy. Should they accomplish the task, the Golden Fleece would be their reward.

The king agreed to his proposal but the task he proposed did not give Jason much hope. He was to yoke two fire oxen of the kings, use them to till the stony field of Ares and then sow the land with the teeth of a dragon. From these teeth, armed men will be born, and Jason will have to confront and kill them all or be killed by them himself.

Despite dire prospects, the leader of the Argonauts did not turn away from this task and decided to entrust his fate in the hands of gods who have, so far, always been at his side.

Jason returned to the ship and once again held the counsel with his men. Argus told him that he could only succeed if he asked the king's daughter and a powerful priestess Medea for help. Jason agreed to this and the next day he met with the priestess.

Medea, who met Jason at the king's banquette, started to develop feelings for him and Jason wasn't indifferent either. Thus, she helped the leader of the Argonauts, giving him a special ointment which turned anyone who used it completely invulnerable to fire and steel for a period of twenty-four hours. She also told him that once the men spring from the dragon teeth, he should throw them a huge rock. They will start to quarrel over ownership of the rock, and their attention will be divided.

Equipped with necessary tools and knowledge, Jason came to the agreed place and performed everything he was tasked with. Once the warriors started appearing from the ground, he threw a huge rock at them, and they immediately started attacking each other. He used their confusion and rushed among them, killing every last one.

When the king saw that his plan failed, he became outraged and not only refused to fulfill his commitment but also turned against the Argonauts, pledging to destroy them all and burn their ship.

Medea, realizing what her father was up to, used the cloak of the night to get on board the Argo and warned the Argonauts their lives were in danger. Then she took Jason with her and led him inside the sacred grove. When they reached the Golden Fleece and the dragon that protected it, the princess used her magic to put the dragon to sleep. Jason used the opportunity and grabbed the Fleece.

Completing his task, Jason took Medea back to the ship, and they set sail immediately. The king, realizing what had happened, sent a large fleet after the Argonauts. After some days at sea, the king's ships finally caught up with Argo and sent messengers, requesting the Argonauts to surrender the princess and the Golden Fleece.

Once again, Medea devised a strategy to save their skins. She tricked her brother, who was leading the fleet, into meeting her during the night, promising to help him reacquire the Fleece. When Absyrtus met her, not suspecting anything, Jason proceeded to kill him, and the Argonauts then attacked the rest of the army, thoroughly defeating them.

The Island of Circe

However, Jason cowardly killing Absyrtus from an ambush was not looked upon kindly by gods, and he was told that he would be free from their wrath only after he had visited goddess Circe and she purified him.

Knowing that the wrath of gods was the one thing they were no match for, the Argonauts set sail to look for the island where Circe lived. Finally arriving at their destination, Jason and Medea paid a visit to the goddess, asking for her protection and purification. Circe indulged their wishes and performed a mystic ritual which saw them both cleansed and their crime forgiven.

Meeting the Sirens and other adventures

Receiving forgiveness for their crime, Jason and Medea commanded Argo to continue her voyage home. On the way back, they passed by the Sirens and were so enchanted by their singing that they almost fell into their trap. Orpheus luckily recognized the danger and used his magic lyre to attract their intention until they were safe.

After avoiding sirens and some other dangers along the way, the Argonauts arrived at the island of the Phaeaces, where they were welcomed by the king and the queen. However, all of a sudden, Medea's father's army appeared, requesting what was his.

At Medea's pleas, the queen Arete decided to offer her assistance. The next day, the assembly of people was gathered, and king Aetes' people were informed that they could not hand over Medea because she was Jason's lawful wife. Fearing the wrath of their king, the army asked for the permission to stay on the island and their request was granted.

The Argonauts faced many more dangers before arriving at the island of Crete, where they briefly stopped to replenish their supplies. Here, yet another challenge awaited them, in a form of a terrifying giant Talus. Talus was the protector of the island and did not look kindly on strangers. The giant was immortal, and his only vulnerable place was his right ankle.

As soon as Talus saw Argo approaching the coast, he started throwing huge rocks at them. Although the crew was desperate for food and fresh water, they decided that the danger was too great and wanted to continue their way, bypassing Crete altogether.

Once again Medea came to the rescue. Using her magic, she invoked the Fates and put the giant to sleep. When he stretched on the ground, he left his right ankle exposed and accidentally hit a sharp rock. A sharp pain woke Talus, but it was too late for him to do anything and he dropped dead on the spot. With the giant out of their way, the Argonauts were free to take the supplies they so desperately needed.

Finally home

After many years of the voyage, the Argonauts finally returned home to Iolcus. Jason took Medea with him and bringing the Golden Fleece, went to greet his uncle Pelias and requested him to fulfill his promise. As expected, Pelias flat out refused Jason's request, as he never intended to honor his word in the first place. He was deeply convinced that the Argonauts would fail.

Medea was deeply insulted by the way her husband was treated and conjured a horrible vengeance. She befriended the king's daughters and told them that she knew the spell to restore one's youth and vigor. To prove her words, Medea cut up an old ram and boiled it in a cauldron. She then proceeded to speak magic words and incantations, and a young lamb appeared from the cauldron. Pelias' daughters, falling for her trick, did the same thing to their father, and became his unwitting murderers.

Jason's death

After her revenge was complete, Medea and Jason fled Iolcus and went to Corinth, where, for a while, they lived happily with their three children. But, with time, Medea's exquisite beauty which charmed Jason started to feign. The famed hero turned his eyes to beautiful Glauce, the king of Corinth's daughter. He even agreed on everything with her father before telling Medea.

However, when Medea was finally informed, no amount of persuasion from Jason could convince her. He tried to explain to her it was just a political alliance and that it would in no way harm their relationship. But the jealous and vengeful priestess would have none of that.

Pretending to understand and accept Jason's reasons, Medea sent a gift to Glauce. It was a majestic cloak but imbued with horrible poison. Unsuspecting Glauce tried the robe as soon as she received it and she perished in dreadful agony.

Medea did not stop at this. Completely crazy because she lost the affection of her husband, she proceeded to kill their three sons and then took off in a golden chariot carried by dragons.

When Jason saw everything that had transpired, it was too much for him to take. The fabled hero fell on his own sword and ended his life which no longer had any purpose.

Chapter Nine - The Siege of Troy

One of the greatest Greek myths is the siege of Troy. No other mythical place in history gathered so many heroes, gods, and demigods, all battling for a common cause but also for their own personal agendas of different natures. We are all well acquainted with stories about mighty Achilles, whose only vulnerable place was his heel and wise Odysseus, who spent many years out at sea, trying to find his way home after the war.

This chapter gives an overview of the heroes of the Trojan War. Who they were, why were they there, and what did they hope to accomplish?

Damming prophecy

Troy was situated in Asia Minor and during the events of the siege, it was governed by the king Priam. Priam was married to Hecuba, daughter of the king of Thrace. They had many children, but the most famous were their two sons, who played a prominent role in the Trojan War: Hector and Paris.

At the day of Paris' birth, Hecuba had a prophetic dream that her younger son would end up bringing the destruction to the city. In hopes of changing the bleak destiny, she brought Paris to Mount Ida and left him there expecting that his life would end.

However, as we've seen time and time again in Greek mythology, gods' designs cannot be altered. Paris was rescued by some shepherds who happened to run into him. The boy was well taken care of and grew up into a good looking and brave young man who protected his benefactors from different perils.

When he became of age, Paris united with the beautiful nymph Enone, and they spent their days in peace, away from the noise and political affairs of the cities. But, at one point, Paris heard about games taking place in Troy and decided to join, completely unaware of his origins.

At the games, he completely defeated his brothers, Hector, and Deiphobus and the young princes were not very happy about. It was a great shame for them to be defeated so by a common shepherd. However, his sister Cassandra, who was a seer, recognized her brother and resolved the dispute. Immediately, everything was forgiven, and great festivities occurred in honor of Paris' return.

Destiny comes to its fruition

With the return of Paris, the destiny which was prophesized could not start to unravel. King Priam decided to entrust his newly found son with a delicate mission of going to Greece and ask the return of his sister who was kidnapped by Hercules and given to his friend Telamon as his wife.

In an effort to save Troy from its dire destiny, Cassandra warned her brother not to bring for himself a wife from Greece under any circumstances. Paris listened to what she had to say and then set sail to Greece to fulfill his father's mission.

Upon arriving in Greece, Paris immediately noticed beautiful Helen, the daughter of Zeus and wife of Spartan king Menelaus. Her beauty was such that many heroes sought her favor but her father, the former king of Sparta, ended up giving her hand to Menelaus, whom he deemed the most worthy.

During Paris' stay at Menelaus' court, the king received an invitation to go hunting and accepted, leaving Helen to entertain the guests. Paris, completely charmed by her beauty and forgetting about all rules of honor, gathered his followers and kidnapped Helen, taking her to his ship and bringing her home to

Troy. Helen herself, although not completely agreeable, was also quite keen on the young and handsome prince.

The announcement of war

Hearing of the horrible treachery that took place under his roof, Menelaus was completely enraged. He and his brother Agamemnon requested the council of the wise king Nestor, who told him that they could only stand a chance against Troy if all Greece stood united.

Greeks responded unanimously, looking to rectify the grave dishonor done to their country. They raised a powerful army which represented a threat even for a kingdom as mighty as Troy. The only two people who had to be convinced to join the cause were Odysseus and Achilles.

Odysseus was reluctant to leave his wife and peaceful life and exchange it for the insecurity and agony of war. However, his ruse to faint madness was uncovered, and he had to join Menelaus in war.

Achilles was the key man for the campaign against Troy. According to a prophecy, Greeks could not succeed without him on their side. Achilles was almost invulnerable, as his mother, the sea goddess Thetis dipped him into the river Styx when he was born. The only vulnerable place on his body was his heel, as this is where Thetis held him, thus preventing the water to come in contact with his skin.

When Achilles was a boy, it was prophesized that he could either live a long life of peace and anonymity or a short one, which would end up in his heroic death. Naturally, wishing to save her son, the goddess dispatched him to the island of Scyros, disguising him as a girl in the company of king Lycomedes' daughters.

Menelaus managed to discover his whereabouts and sent Odysseus on a mission to bring Achilles with him. Using his wisdom and deception, Odysseus discovered the hero among the girls and he willingly joined the cause. At the request of his father, the hero Peleus, he was accompanied by his cousin Patroclus and an army of Thessalian forces (myrmidons).

After they gathered heroes from all corners of Greece, Menelaus, and his brother started preparing a large fleet of ships for departure. It took them ten years during which they also tried to come up with a peaceful resolution. Menelaus, accompanied by Odysseus and several other renown heroes went to king Priam, asking for Helen to be returned to them. Despite a friendly welcome in Troy, their demands eventually fell on deaf ears, and the war was the only remaining option.

After they had offered sacrifices to gods, Greeks set sail for Troy. They received a sign that the war would last for nine full years and that only in the tenth year Troy would fall. Their journey was a lengthy one, filled with adventures and conflicts with gods, especially goddess Artemis because Agamemnon accidentally killed her sacred hind. In the end, they were able to put all this behind them and finally arrived in Troy.

The siege begins

Spotting the Greek fleet, Trojans gathered on the coast hoping to prevent their landing. The band of the greatest heroes of Greece, leading a big number of ordinary troops, managed to thoroughly defeat the Trojan army, forcing them behind the walls of the city and recording the first victory in the war that would last a full decade.

However, Greeks quickly realized that they could not storm the fortified city of Troy. Their first attempt was met with great resistance, and many of their men fell in the skirmish. Trojans, who were fewer in numbers, knew that they stood no chance if they faced the enemy in an open field and so the stalemate began.

Unable to attack Troy directly, Greeks spent the first year pillaging the nearby villages. During one such attack, they conquered and sacked the city of Pedasus and as a reward, Achilles received the beautiful Briseis, while Agamemnon took for himself Chryseis, the daughter of Chryes, who was Apollo's priest.

The next day Chryses came to beg for his daughter to be returned to him but was laughed away by Agamemnon. The old man, filled with grief and feeling of powerlessness, raised his voice to Apollo. The god, hearing the prayer of his priest, sent upon Greeks a terrible pestilence which killed many of them.

Achilles offended

The seer Calchas explained to them the reasons behind the pestilence and Agamemnon agreed to return the girl to her father. However, he also accused the seer that he was plotting against him. Achilles took Calchas side in the argument and had goddess Athena not intervened Achilles would have probably ended up killing Agamemnon. Menelaus' brother was deeply offended by this behavior and took Briseis away from Achilles, thus punishing him for his rebellious behavior.

Achilles was now very distressed and sought the help of his mother, goddess Thetis. She told him she would beg Zeus to award the victory to Trojans, thus punishing the Greeks for their offense. When the word of Achilles departure reached the Trojans, they immediately launched an attack against the Greeks and started recording one victory after another, forcing the Greek army all the way back to their camp.

Agamemnon, seeing that they were inches away from complete destruction, sent messengers to Achilles, apologizing for earlier grievances and promising that everything would be set right. Achilles wouldn't listen to these pleas and remained determined to no longer participate in the war.

The Trojans continued defeating the Greeks and were already at the heart of their camp. Patroclus then begged Achilles to at least let him lead Myrmidons to assist the fellow Greeks. The hero relented and even gave his armor to Patroclus to wear it in the battle.

Seeing Patroclus approach with the troops, Trojans mistook him for Achilles because of the armor he was wearing, and fled the camp. However, Patroclus was not satisfied with this and kept chasing the enemy all the way to the gates of Troy. Here, he encountered Hector, the son of Priam, who took his life.

Hector's death

Hearing of the fate of his dear friend, Achilles vowed that no funeral rites would take place until Patroclus death was avenged. Putting aside his quarrels with Agamemnon, Achilles once again joined the Greek army. He received a new armor from the god Hephaestus, as his old one was taken by Hector and he proceeded to the gates of Troy to challenge Hector to a duel.

Seeing Achilles in all his might and fury, for the first time in his life, Hector felt afraid for his life and started fleeing. The Greek hero pursued him around the city, as Hector tried to find refuge inside the walls. In the end, seeing that he could not escape enraged Achilles, Hector stood his ground and faced his adversary one to one, only to be slain in the short battle that ensued.

Achilles then proceeded to violate Hector's body, dragging it around the city tied to his chariot. After he was done with his revenge, he proceeded to give Patroclus a funeral he deserved, followed by funeral games held in his honor.

Amazons to the rescue

After the death of Hector, the Trojans were disheartened and for the most part stayed within the walls of their city. But one day an army of Amazons appeared, led by their queen Penthesilea. She heard the stories of mighty Achilles and was informed about the horrible fate that fell upon Hector and was there seeking revenge.

The Trojans gained new courage and joined the Amazons in yet another attempt against the Greeks. Once again they were defeated but Penthesilea, a daughter of the god Ares himself, challenged Achilles to a duel. Although a brave warrior herself, the Amazon queen was no match for the hero and like many others before her, she was sent to the realm of shadows.

Achilles' death

Although the Trojans were defeated in battle once again, their city still stood firm. After some time, a new ally of theirs appeared. It was Memnon, who brought with him another army and who was the only person in the entire Trojan army who could stand against Achilles. Memnon too was a son of a goddess and had a special armor made by Hephaestus.

Eventually, the two heroes met in the duel and yet again, Achilles emerged victoriously. Drunken with success and on the wings of this victory, the hero led the Greek army in another attempt to storm Troy. Paris, standing on the city walls and helped by Apollo, sent an arrow through the air, hitting one vulnerable spot on Achilles' entire body - his heel.

Thus ended the greatest Greek hero, not in a duel against his equal, but pierced by a treacherous arrow, sent at him from the safety of the city walls.

The end of siege

Having lost their biggest and most courageous hero, the Greeks fell into desperation. Then Odysseus came up with the plan to capture Helenus, another son of Priam, who, like his sister, was able to see the future.

Forced to work against his own countrymen, unfortunate Helenus told them that if they were to capture Troy, they had to meet three conditions:

- The son of Achilles must fight in their ranks;

- The arrows of Hercules must be used;

- They must capture the wooden image of the goddess Athena, the renowned Palladium of Troy

Odysseus took it upon himself to meet the first two conditions and retrieved Achilles' son Neoptolemus from the island of Scyros and retrieved the poisoned arrows of Hercules. However, if they wanted to have any chance of succeeding, they still needed the Palladium of Troy.

Once again, Odysseus used his cunning and managed to enter the city disguised as a beggar. No one recognized Odysseus inside the town, except for Helen but after her husband Paris was killed by the poisoned arrow, her hurt once again turned to her fellow countrymen. With some difficulty, he managed to retrieve the Palladium and now all conditions were met for the destruction of Troy.

The Trojan horse

With all conditions fulfilled, all they needed now was to get behind the city walls. To achieve this, they come up with an idea to construct a big wooden horse and hide inside it the bravest Greek warriors. Then, they would leave the horse on the shore and pretend to leave, tricking Trojans into believing they gave up and that the horse was left behind as a sign of their surrender.

Trojans fell for their ruse and brought the horse inside the gates despite some being against it. One of the most vocal was Laocoon, Apollo's priest, who pierced the horse's side with a lance, wounding one of the warriors inside. When the Greeks started thinking it was all lost, Athena surged to their help, performing a miracle and convincing the Trojans the horse was sacred and they should take it inside the city.

Furthering their conviction was the Greek Sinon, whom Odysseus left behind with very specific instructions. He convinced the Trojans that the horse was an offering to the goddess Athena and that the Greeks have betrayed him and tried to sacrifice him before leaving.

King Priam and others fell for the story and allowed Sinon to enter Troy together with the wooden horse which would mark the end of the city. Cassandra was the only one who saw that something was wrong with the horse and tried to warn the Trojans, but no one would listen as it was destined for Troy to fall.

When feasting and celebrating was over inside Troy, under the veil of night, Sinon opened the hidden door on the horse and released the heroes into the city. The Greek army, which was hiding nearby, once again returned to the coast and silently approached Troy. The heroes opened the gates from inside and let inside the Greek army, marking the final moments of the city.

During the attack, king Priam himself fell by the hand of Neoptolemus, who killed him at the altar of Zeus. Menelaus found Helen, who, being immortal was still as beautiful as ever and the two reconciled.

Priam's wife Hecuba became the prisoner of Odysseus, while Paris' sister Cassandra belonged to Agamemnon. The Greeks proceeded to pillage and rob Troy of its immense wealth before finally sailing back home after ten long years of battle.

Thus fell the city of Troy and destiny was fulfilled.

Conclusion

There is something about Greek mythology which has captured the minds and hearts of many people all over the world. Even before the time of Homer, the myths of the gods were both entertaining and educational. For centuries, the myths of the gods and goddesses were the source of inspiration for artists of all kinds, to politicians and philosophers, all of whom used the ancient stories to explain the natural world, explain social customs, why they were going to war etc.

Greek mythology is a great source of inspiration when it comes to history and archaeology. Whilst myths are fantastical stories, rich in imaginative details, they also offer us an interesting glimpse into the history of Greece before the written language was introduced. The stories of the Trojan War appear to have been an actual fact, although perhaps not quite as according to Homer's poems, and the palace of Knossos highlights an advanced civilization living on Crete.

No other civilization has a mythological background as rich and inspiring as that of ancient Greece. Even today, the myths of Greek god, goddesses, heroes and monsters are still the source of inspiration of many artists including painters, novelists and movie producers. There is little doubt that even in centuries to come, Greek myths will still continue to inspire.

Printed in Great Britain
by Amazon